When I came to Oxford as a young doctor I found myself surrounded by Nuffield, his benefactions had transformed the entire environment. But William Morris, later Lord Nuffield, transformed not simply Oxford Medicine, but the entire city of Oxford, and so much more. He became one of the most influential philanthropists of his time, whose generous gifts have had lasting National and International impact.

David Cranston and Peter Morris tell the fascinating story of how this unpretentious, enigmatic man became one of the foremost industrial figures and philanthropists of the 20th century. The work interleaves the story of Nuffield the man with a compelling account of the challenges, opportunities, up and downs of his times. Read and enjoy.

Professor Sir Peter Ratcliffe FRS, FMedSci,
Nuffield Professor of Medicine 2014-2016 and
Clinical Research Director at the Francis Crick Institute, London

While the status of Lord Nuffield as one of the most successful industrialists and his reputation as one of the most generous philanthropist of his time are well known, this short and very clear account of his life also draws attention to a person and a career with very humble beginnings, less known, but delightfully explored in this illustrated book.

Pierre Foex, FMedSci,
Emeritus Nuffield Professor of Anaesthetics, University of Oxford

An incisive and comprehensive account of the extraordinary life of William Morris, Lord Nuffield. A rags to riches journey culminating in some of the most remarkable philanthropy of the twentieth century.

Professor Andy Carr, FMedSci,
Nuffield Professor of Orthopaedic Surgery Oxford

Having worked at Nuffield Place, now owned by the National Trust, Lord Nuffield's home from 1933-1963 for over 40 years, I have read most of what is available to read about Lord Nuffield. I read this book with great enjoyment because he has put together the facts we know in such a way as to create a lively and interesting story, stuffed with facts, anecdotes and quotes from the man himself. I highly recommend this book to all those who are interested in the Nuffield story – one of the most important stories of the 20th century.

Joanna Gamester,
House Steward, Nuffield Place

Lord Nuffield
and his
Double Legacy

Lord Nuffield
and his
Double Legacy

David Cranston and Peter Morris
Illustrated by Valerie Petts

William Morris, Lord Nuffield (copy after Philip Alexius de László)
Reginald Henry Lewis (1894–1973)
Green Templeton College, University of Oxford

David Cranston *completed his medical training in Bristol and worked in Exeter and Bath before coming to Oxford for post-graduate doctoral research. He is a Fellow of the Royal College of Surgeons of England and is Honorary Consultant Urological Surgeon in the Oxford University Hospitals NHS Trust, Associate Professor of Surgery in the Nuffield Department of Surgical Science and a Fellow of Green Templeton College, Oxford and joint curator of 13 Norham Gardens. Outside medicine he serves as a licensed lay minister in the Church of England and is on the board of the Oxford Centre for Mission Studies.*

Professor Sir **Peter Morris**, *an Australian, is Nuffield Professor of Surgery Emeritus, and former Chairman of the Department of Surgery and Director of the Oxford Transplant Centre, Emeritus Fellow Balliol College and past President of the Royal College of Surgeons of England. He was appointed from the University of Melbourne to the Nuffield Chair at Oxford in 1973 at the age of 39. He was elected as a Fellow of the Royal Society in 1994 and as a Foundation Fellow of the Academy of Medical Sciences in 1998. In the USA he was elected as a Foreign Member of both the National Academy of Medicine and the American Philosophical Society. He has been awarded numerous Honorary Fellowships of Surgical and Medical Colleges throughout the world. In addition he has been awarded Honorary DSc's by Imperial College, London and the University of Hong Kong, and an Honorary Doctorate of Laws, University of Melbourne. He has published over 700 scientific articles and is among the 200 most cited authors in clinical medicine worldwide. In 1996 he was knighted by the Queen for services to medicine and in 2004 was made a Companion of the Order of Australia (the highest award in Australia) for services to medical sciences.*

Valerie Petts *first started training as a lab technician in Professor Howard Florey's department in Oxford before working in clinical immunology research in London and Sydney and has been painting full-time since about 1990. She has had numerous exhibitions in England and has also exhibited in Tokyo and Cape Town. She has illustrated five books including* Oxford Words and Watercolours, Consider England, John Radcliffe and his Legacy to Oxford, Penicillin and the Legacy of Norman Heatley, *and a visitors' book for the National Trust.*

FOREWORD

This is the story of William Morris, later Lord Nuffield.

Early in his life Morris became interested in transport on bicycles and motorbikes and other forms of transport, and later in the development of cars. He developed a series of brilliant cars and developed one of the largest motor companies in the country. Over the years he became extremely rich.

Morris was extremely generous with his money in a whole variety of directions. Later as Lord Nuffield he became particularly generous to Oxford University in many directions including the establishment of the Medical School, developing buildings for medical research, providing senior medical staff, helping to develop all the hospitals in Oxford, and much more.

It is a pity that Lord Nuffield did not survive to a later phase in the development of Oxford's Medical School. If he had he would have read that over recent years Oxford has been the top Medical School in the world. In each of those years the published figures show that Oxford is followed in its excellence by Harvard Medical School and leads Harvard by half a percent!

Although quite a lot has been written over the years about the life and generosity of Lord Nuffield, little has been presented in such detail as portrayed here by the present authors, who should be congratulated.

David Weatherall GBE MD FRCP FRS
Regius Professor of Medicine Emeritus
University of Oxford

ACKNOWLEDGEMENTS

We are grateful to Professor David Weatherall for his foreword and to Professors Andy Carr, Pierre Foex and Peter Ratcliffe for their commendations. Valerie Petts has enhanced the book tremendously by her beautiful watercolours, while Tony Gray has been very helpful and patient as both editor and publisher through his company WORDS BY DESIGN.

Picture Credits

v, 12, 13, 17a, 19, 23, 28, 29, 36, 38, 56, 72, 88, 92, 94. Peter Morris collection

84, 93. Words by Design

2. http://www.bullnose.org.uk/articles/william-richard-morris-lord-nuffield/

7. https://www.etsy.com/uk/listing/191428246/victorian-women-bicycle-riders-1890s

8. https://velojoy.com/2011/06/15/bike-skirt-strife-sells-both-women-and-men-short/

14. http://www.oxfordhistory.org.uk/high/tour/north/048.html

15. https://www.gracesguide.co.uk/Oxford_Automobile_and_Cycle_Agency

17b. http://www.oxfordhistory.org.uk/mayors/1836_1962/cavell_john_1865_1879.html

22. William Osler and His Legacy to Medicine

30. http://www.oxfordhistory.org.uk/high/history/transport_1905.html

32a. https://www.arnoldclark.com/newsroom/046-oxford-s-cowley-plant-celebrates-a-century-of-car-making

32b. https://www.bbc.co.uk/news/uk-england-oxfordshire-21942941

34. By Unknown – Sjöhistoriska museet, Public Domain, https://commons.wikimedia.org/w/index.php?curid=42989236

35. https://morrisbearings.co.uk

42. https://www.mgabingdon.org.uk/mg-timeline/

44. https://www.gracesguide.co.uk/File:Im19291011LC-Morris.jpg

50. By Lonpicman [CC BY-SA 3.0 (https://creativecommons.org/licenses/by-sa/3.0) or GFDL (http://www.gnu.org/copyleft/fdl.html)], from Wikimedia Commons

55a, 55b. http://www.controltowers.co.uk/C/Cowley.html

55c. http://www.wellingtont2905.co.uk/story.html

57. http://www.alternativefinland.com/british-tanks-inter-war-decades/

59. https://www.telegraph.co.uk/motoring/8236614/The-Morris-Minor-A-British-miracle.html

60. https://www.gracesguide.co.uk/Morris:_Cars

62. http://vscca.org.au/mg-reg-rep-6-10.html

68. http://hauntedearthghostvideos.blogspot.com/2012/04/ghostly-history-of-radcliffe-infirmary.html

70. http://www.headington.org.uk/history/streets/windmill_road/11_wingfield.html

76. Penicillin and the Legacy of Norman Heatley

79. https://www.silvertraveladvisor.com/review/attraction/163716-nuffield-place-national-trust-interesting-few-hours

84. Words by Design

89. http://www.headington.org.uk/history/famous_people/nuffield.htm

Dedication

To our wives, Rosie and Joce

CONTENTS

Foreword   vii
Acknowledgements   ix
Contents   xiii
Introduction   xv

1	Beginnings	1
2	Bicycles	5
3	Early Ventures in Motoring	15
4	Motor Cars	23
5	The First World War	35
6	Between the Wars	39
7	The Second World War	53
8	Post-War Consolidation	59
9	Morris' Benefactions	65
10	Nuffield the Man	87

Further Reading   95
Appendix: Morris Cars   97

INTRODUCTION

William Morris' legacy is immense. From mending bicycles in the house of his parents to becoming the motoring giant of the UK where the MG insignia (Morris Garages) is universally known sixty years after his death... not to mention the two war efforts in which he played a major role, rebuilding the RAF several times over especially during the crucial days of the Battle of Britain in 1940. His interest in, and philanthropy toward, medicine in particular may have been stimulated by his early connections with Sir William Osler, who was Regius Professor of Medicine in Oxford between 1905 and 1919. He endowed the four original Nuffield Chairs of Medicine, Surgery, Obstetrics and Gynaecology, Anaesthetics, and a few years later Orthopaedics. One of the authors (PJM) held the Nuffield Chair of Surgery between 1974 and 2001 stimulating his long-term interest in William Morris. Ennobled as Lord Nuffield in 1934, this book uses both 'William Morris' and 'Nuffield' or 'Lord Nuffield' when referring to him (mainly but not exclusively 'Morris' before 1934 and 'Nuffield' after 1934).

CHAPTER 1: BEGINNINGS

William Richard Morris was born on 10th October 1877 in 47 Comer Gardens, Worcester, England, a small terraced house two miles from the town centre. He died 85 years later on 22nd August 1963. He was to make his name as one of the great British industrialists and car makers, and was the greatest British philanthropist of the twentieth century. He left his mark for ever on the British motor industry and the Oxford Medical School, in addition to his countless gifts and legacies in so many different areas.

His ancestors can be traced back to 1278. All had been small farmers in Oxfordshire and William Morris was the first to be born outside the county. His father, Frederick Morris, was born in Oxford and was a senior boy at Hurst's Grammar School, Cowley. On a number of occasions while there, he thought another boy was being unjustly punished. One day he could stand it no longer and arose from his place in class to knock the master down. He then fled home and after talking the matter over with his parents, decided that his education had come to an end and so emigrated to Canada. There he became an expert horseman and learned to drive a Royal Mail coach with six horses between Winnipeg and Toronto. It was a time when the native Canadians were numerous and Royal Canadian Mounted Police few! He is also said to have spent time trapping and prospecting and, indeed, would entertain the young William for hours on end with stories of his encounters with the natives and how he had become a blood brother and an honorary chief of one of the native tribes in Canada.

Frederick decided to return home and in 1876 he married Emily Ann Pether, daughter of Richard Pether of Wood Farm, Headington in Oxford, and they set up home in Worcester where William was born. Throughout his life he was always known as William or Will, or by his initials WRM, and never Bill which he disliked.

In Worcester, his father Frederick worked for a draper, but having farming and an open country life in his blood, he did not take to it easily and returned to Oxford in 1880 to make

1896, when Morris was 19, standing behind his parents Frederick and Emily Morris, along with his sisters Alice (standing) and Emily

the family home at 16 James Street. Here Frederick Morris became bailiff to his father-in-law, Mr Pepper, who farmed at Headington Quarry but had gone blind. However, later episodes of asthma forced Frederick to take a clerical job to support his family of seven, of whom William was the eldest.

Will was educated at the church school in Cowley until the age of 14. Outside school hours (and occasionally within them), he would occupy himself in fishing, rambling and cycling through the countryside. On at least one occasion he received a punishment from the headmaster after he arrived back an hour late for afternoon school, having prolonged his midday break fishing.

CHAPTER 2: BICYCLES

When he was 14 Morris taught himself to ride a borrowed penny farthing bike and afterwards put his savings into a second-hand bike which had solid tyres, the first bicycle he owned.

He would often ride with one or two friends along the Garsington Road, which in those days was a rough track with high hedges and a high grass verge. Sometimes the trips were further afield, and on one occasion he went cycling with a friend to London and left the bicycles with a shopkeeper on Oxford Street. However, when they came to return they were unable to remember where they had left them and had to ask a policeman to help find them.

By the time William Morris and his friends were struggling to mount their first penny farthings in the leafy lanes of Cowley, the bicycle had been around for half a century. In 1818 the German Baron, Karl von Drais, invented the hobbyhorse shaped like a bicycle with wooden wheels, although it had no pedals so that the rider had to push it along with their feet. Initially it was the height of fashion among rich young men, but the craze ended when the Royal College of Surgeons in London warned that it could cause 'ruptures'.

More conventional bicycle production had started in the 1860s in France, when Pierre Michaux and his son Ernest converted a hobbyhorse by the addition of pedals, and by the mid-1860s they were turning out 400 a year in their workshop near Verdun. Michaux organised a women's race to advertise the new bicycle, but when the female riders appeared in short skirts the crowd of 3,000 burst through the barriers. Undaunted, the women sped off, an early demonstration of how bicycles were to liberate their sex. British engineers improved on Michaux's design by adding wire spoke wheels and rubber tyres, reducing the overall weight, but in the absence of gears they could only increase the speed by making the front wheel bigger, which is how the penny farthing evolved. However, the seat of the penny farthing was high, making it difficult to climb onto and dangerous to fall off. It required physical agility to mount and control a penny farthing machine, let alone ride any distance on the appalling roads of the time. In 1885 the Rover safety bicycles launched the first model to adopt what is now the standard bicycle design with the lower seating and a chain to drive the back wheel, making it safe, practical and fast.

When the bicycle went into mass production in the 1890s it was the most revolutionary form of transport ever invented at the time. It enlarged the human gene pool, for people no longer had to marry the girl or boy next door, but could get onto their bicycle and pedal to the next village or town, or even further afield, to find a partner. Within two decades almost every working man in Britain owned a bike, revolutionising the day-to-day life for the middle and working classes – for instead of having to live in overcrowded inner-city tenements, they were now able to commute from newly built suburbs.

In 1896 the American suffragist Susan Anthony said the bicycle had done more to emancipate women than anything else in the world. Previously women were restricted not just socially and legally but physically, confined to the home with tight corsets and unwieldy skirts that hampered any movement. The bicycle changed all this. It allowed women to get out and about, often without chaperones, improving their health and encouraging new modes of dress. Not everyone approved and when some early female cyclists were pictured

Two Victorian women ready to cycle

on the front of the National Police Gazette it caused a scandal, with the outraged headline, 'She wore trousers!' Doctors warned that unusual physical exertion combined with the lack of corsetry would damage 'the feminine organs of matrimonial necessity'!

Flora Thompson, in her book *Lark Rise to Candleford*, has a captivating description of the bicycling scene of the 1880s:

The first high 'penny-farthing' bicycles were already on the roads, dancing and swerving like swallows heralding the summer of the buses and cars and motorcycles which were soon to transform country life. But how fast those new bicycles travelled and how dangerous they looked! Pedestrians backed up almost into the hedges when they met one of them, for was there not almost every week in the Sunday newspapers the story of someone being knocked down and killed by the bicycle, and letters from readers saying cyclists ought to not to be allowed to use the roads, which, as everyone knew, were provided for people to walk on or to drive on behind horses. 'Bicyclists ought to have roads to themselves, like railway trains' was the general opinion.

Yet it was thrilling to see a man hurtling through space on one high wheel with another tiny wheel wobbling helplessly behind. You wondered how they managed to keep their balance. No wonder they wore an anxious air. 'Bicyclist's face', the expression was called, and the newspapers foretold a hunchbacked and tortured-faced future generation as a result of the pastime.

Cycling was looked upon as a passing craze and the cyclists in their tight navy knickerbocker suits and pillbox caps with the badge of their club in front were regarded as figures of fun. None of those in the hamlet would have believed, if they had been told, that in a few years there would be at least one bicycle in every one of their houses, that the men would ride to work on them and the younger women, when their housework was done, would lightly mount 'the old bike' and pedal away to the market town to see the shops. They would have been still more incredulous had they been told that many of them would live to see every child of school age in the hamlet provided by a kind County Council with a bicycle on which they would ride to school, 'all free, gratis, and for nothing'.

By 1880 there were about 230 cycle clubs in the United Kingdom and a textbook for riders, written in 1874, set out the details of various cycling routes. One of their first targets for them was lobbying for an improvement of the roads. Some roads were good, but others were full of holes and described as rutty and uneven. The cyclist of today may sometimes think that not much has changed! The pneumatic tyre was patented by Dunlop in 1888, and another by Michelin four years later, which smoothed the ride considerably.

The mid-1890s witnessed a bicycle boom and the number of firms involved multiplied year by year, and it was into this market that the young William now entered. His father's ill health prevented him from continuing his education and he left school to find a job to help support the family – his duty as the eldest son. He did not regret the move, saying,

From that date the workshop appeared to me infinitely more attractive than the school room.

The only other education he ever received was at an engineering evening class, but he only attended twice and did not find it very useful. Otherwise he was completely self-taught, learning from trade journals and engineering manuals. He never regarded formal high-level training as being of any great value for his business career or those of his executives saying:

I've lived long enough to know that it is not always the men who have an expensive education that do things.

He had always enjoyed working with his hands, and his sister remembers him constructing a model bicycle and making her a penknife out of discarded pieces of other knives. Early on in his career William heard that the linotype machine used by the Oxford Times had broken down. A split had developed in parts of a cast iron slide. No replacements could be found, and the newspaper was dependent on this for its printing. William Morris offered his help, arriving the day before the paper was due to go to press… but he was not well received by the foreman who was sceptical about the value of the help they would get from such a young man. Nevertheless, Morris persuaded the foreman to let him see the damage and decided it needed brazing and offered to do it. Brazing is a process in which two or more metal items are

joined together by melting and allowing a filler metal with a lower melting point to run into the join and then harden on cooling. William took the parts away and four hours later returned with it repaired. The machine continued to work until it was scrapped in 1937.

In 1892 he began working in a bicycle repair shop in Oxford. He kept a list of all the repairs he did and was paid for his keep, but after nine months realised that he was earning his keep several times over and asked the boss for a shilling a week rise. When this was refused he handed in his resignation, and decided that,

> No one will pay me wages as high as Will Morris, so I'll work for him.

Having saved £4 over the previous nine months, he set up in business for himself in a shed at the back of their home in James Street. Initially his father called him, "the biggest fool you could possibly think of", but it wasn't long after that he changed his mind! His mother, on the other hand, encouraged him in what he did, always leaving him free to follow his inclinations.

The £4 provided the tools he needed and very quickly his business started to boom. It was not long before he started building bicycles as well as repairing them. At that point he took over one of the front rooms of the house as a display area for his own bicycles. The first bicycle he made was at the request of the Rector of St Clement's Church in Oxford, a Mr Pilcher. He was a large man and asked for a 27-inch bicycle frame. Forty-four years later Morris bought it back, still in good condition, and so showing the outstanding quality of his early work. The only parts that needed replacing were the cork handle grip and one small pivot screw in the brake lever. It had been used daily by the Rector and provided a good advertisement for Morris, whose reputation was further improved by the personal recommendation of Mr Pilcher.

In 1896-7 Morris was listed as one of 16 cycle makers and agents in Kelly's Directory for Oxford. Most of his cycle parts were supplied from Birmingham and on occasions he would cycle 120 miles there and back in a day to collect parts, then working late into the night to complete jobs.

By the end of the 1890s he had outgrown the house in James Street and moved to Harold Field's shop, 48 High Street, Oxford. Here, in what he described as the most beautiful street in the world, he was to assemble his bicycles, labelling his product with a gilt cycle wheel and his logo 'The Morris'.

The first bicycle made by Morris in 1893

As a manufacturer of bicycles, he decided the best way to prove the superiority of his model was to race it. In his first race in 1897 he was unplaced, having just had all his teeth out after years of neglect and a bad anaesthetic. However, over the following years he became champion of three counties, Oxford, Berkshire and Buckinghamshire, for distances varying between one and fifty miles. There is this impressive picture of him in black singlet and skullcap, although it was apparently taken with him stationary, and the person holding the bicycle was subsequently painted out of the picture.

He decided to retire from competitive cycling in 1901 at the age of 24 having won the title the two previous years. However, in 1904 a younger generation founded the 'Oxford Wheelers' and resurrected the championships. Thinking that Morris would not compete again, they asked him to return his cups. They were mistaken, for he knew that if he won the cups for a third time he could keep them for good. He practised on little-used roads, unknown to his competitors, and in the mile race he led from the start and won by twenty yards. In the fifty-mile race which followed almost immediately, he would introduce irregular bursts of speed which served to upset his opponents, and each burst of speed resulted in the withdrawal of one of the other six entrants. After 17 miles the race was stopped in favour of Morris, as he was the only competitor left. Having won three times he was able to keep both cups outright. He never raced again.

On one occasion Morris took some new racing bikes to London to be exhibited at the annual show in Islington. He was up all night for several nights to finish them, and on the way down was so tired that he fell asleep on the Underground Circle Line. Eventually a porter at one of the stations had to shake him awake after he had passed the same station four times! He managed to get the cycles onto the stand with five minutes to spare before the 10.00 pm deadline.

48 High Street premises

14

Chapter 3: Early Ventures in Motoring

Much of the technology involved in making bicycles, including the pneumatic tyre, was later used in the manufacture of cars. All the leading car makers made bicycles before they made cars. It was the cycling groups that lobbied for smooth asphalt roads to be laid down all over the country, paving the way for the car – something which may never have happened if the bicycle had not come first.

However, Morris' first venture into motor manufacturing was the motorcycle, and by mounting an engine onto one of his solidly made bicycles he made his first experimental motorcycle. Before long he was producing the Morris Motor Cycle with 2¾ horsepower engines. Yet it was to be the motor car that fired his imagination.

In 1885, Karl Benz developed a petrol or gasoline-powered automobile, considered to be the first 'production' vehicle, as Benz had made several other identical copies. In the 1890s cars were the playthings of the rich and steam cars refuelled at the village ponds, disturbing ducks and cows.

The Red Flag Act, introduced in 1865, stunted the growth of British motor industry by insisting that a man with a red flag should walk in front of every 'horseless carriage' and limit their speed to 2 mph in urban areas. This was repealed in 1896 and was a sign to those who had made fortunes out of the bicycle to try their hand at car manufacture. Yet despite their enthusiasm, the British were ten years behind the Germans and French.

Many still felt that although the motor car would not dislodge the place of the fashionable trotting pony and trap, it might end the struggle of horses straining to pull heavy omnibuses and drays, and also protect the plight of the thoroughbreds whose racing days were over and who ended their days pulling cabs (rather than in a field enjoying a quiet well-earned retirement).

In 1903 at the age of 14 Alfred Keen joined Morris and was to stay with him for the rest of his working life. He originally had plans to be apprenticed in Reading, but it would have cost him £10 and so instead an uncle in the Oxford police force suggested he work for Morris where he earned two shillings and sixpence a week. Alfred was later one of three non-family members to have special bequests made to them in Morris' will. Morris had a knack of picking and keeping good men who worked long hours without overtime pay for the interest of the job.

On 9th April 1903 Morris married Elizabeth Maud Anstey. Known as Lilian, she was the daughter of a farrier who had

Elizabeth Maud Anstey, and an advert for Elliston & Cavell's where she worked

left his wife and family when Lilian was aged 16, to go and live in Leeds where he had a post with the university. His daughters worked to support themselves, the oldest and youngest becoming teachers, while Lilian worked in the Oxford department store, *Elliston & Cavell's*, as a dressmaker. In the 1980s there were still those who could recall having their school uniform made by Miss Anstey.

William Morris and Lilian Anstey had met through cycling. All three of the Anstey women had joined a cycling club at which Morris was also a member. In fact, two of the three met their husbands there. It was a touring club, more sedate than the fierce racing in which Morris had previously been engaged, but the members went on lengthy rides together. Lilian was a strong and tall young lady and she and William would often be seen riding a tandem together. Even though the roads were in poor condition, members of the club often went for longer trips for the weekend, sometimes as far afield as Brighton, over 100 miles away. On several occasions William and Lilian would even go over the Welsh mountains to Aberystwyth and back for their weekends.

They married in 1904 just as William's business collapsed. Several years earlier in 1900 a well-to-do Oxford undergraduate and another businessman approached him with a proposal to go into partnership. Morris agreed, and the Oxford Automobile and Cycle Agency was formed, with the idea that they would continue to sell bicycles as well as automobiles. Morris blamed the business collapse on the reckless spending of the undergraduate. It is alleged that he always was highly suspicious of university graduates thereafter and, indeed, would not employ any university graduate in his business for many years. The collapse left Morris with debts of £50 and he had to stand in the rain to buy back his own tools in the auction which followed. Despite the collapse he retained the goodwill of both his customers and suppliers and retained his reputation of being the best technical man in Oxford. He began with a new determination and resolved that he would put all his money into production (not promotion), and that he would never again enter into a partnership with anyone else.

He never forgot the support his new wife gave him at that moment when his business was in ruins. It was said that she sold all her jewellery (except a wedding ring) to help keep themselves afloat. Years later he told Dr Christopher Chavasse, the Bishop of Rochester, who was raising money for St Peter's Hall in Oxford, that nobody could have a better wife than he did at that time when he had been fighting for his professional life. However, it reinforced his wife's belief in the uncertainty of life and went some way to explaining the reputation she had, later in life, of extreme caution with money – which some would describe as meanness. She was always frightened that the same thing would happen again.

On one occasion the couple had a somewhat narrow escape in the car. When driving just north of Oxford, toward Kidlington, the car brakes failed on the level crossing at Strathfield Brake. A signalman was able to put detonators on the railway line and fortunately the train stopped just five yards away from the car without damaging it. By then the two occupants had made their escape but were watching apprehensively to see if their car was going to be hit.

In 1906 Morris started a car hire business and then combined this with a taxi service, hiring out both the car and the driver. George Tobin joined as a driver in 1906 and had a

The Longwall Garage with hire cars and drivers, 1907.
This is where the first motorbike was also produced.

great deal of respect for Morris, calling him 'uncle' (although not to his face). He reported that Morris would be in the workshop with the rest of them with his old blue overalls on, "Just a mechanic like ourselves... he really was an honest-to-goodness workman and a clever mechanic, there is no question about it."

In 1906 a general election was due and the candidates who could afford it wanted a motor car to help travel around their constituencies. As a result, motor cars were very difficult to come by. One candidate in Scotland, failing to obtain a car locally, looked further afield and contacted Morris, having heard of his reputation. However, Morris had no cars available at the time but suggested he might obtain one from Paris, and it was agreed that he should go there to see if he could secure one. Morris left for Paris the same night and eventually, after some searching, found a dealer who had a Lacoste & Batmen car to sell. He bought it and on New Year's Day 1906 started his long drive home.

After 25 miles the car broke down, the gearbox and axle drive seizing in freezing temperatures due to lack of oil and grease. With no hope of a local repair, Morris took the train back to Paris to get spares which he had pay for as there was no warranty on the car. After repairing it himself, he set off again but at midnight the exhaust valve broke, although for this he had a spare. However, it was an eighth of an inch too long, so Morris ground it down on the cobblestones, fitted it, and reached Oxford on 5th January.

The next day he sent the car north with Alfred Keen and a driver. As the two of them reached York the back axle broke. Morris travelled up to York and repaired the car in the nearby blacksmith's shop. The same problem occurred at Berwick-on-

Tweed, calling for the removal of the back axle of the car in freezing darkness. In order to repair it, Morris worked for twelve hours without sleep. Setting off again on 8th January they arrived at their destination after dark, and as they entered the drive of the candidate's house, the propeller shaft seized! They were greeted by the candidate coming back from a meeting in a horse-drawn carriage, followed by a demand for an immediate explanation of the delay. The following day the back axle was taken down again. It was beyond repair and Morris went to Edinburgh where replacements were made and on 11th January the car was repaired. Morris took the candidate for his first drive and returning home the propeller shaft seized once more. The candidate had to make his own way home!

The candidate's complaint was understandable, but because this had cost Morris a great deal of time and money, not to say frustration, he told the candidate that he either paid for the car, or the order should be cancelled and he would take the car away and sell it elsewhere. The gentleman chose to buy it and that was the last Morris ever heard of it.

It was around this time that Morris met William Osler in Oxford and formed an association that would become of great significance in later years. William Osler was the most famous physician of his day. A Canadian by birth who had moved to America to become one of the founding fathers of the Johns Hopkins Hospital, at the close of his career Osler was appointed Regius Professor of Medicine in Oxford.

Although the motor car was not a form of transport in which Osler's wife, Grace, took great pleasure, it did make it easy to reach otherwise inaccessible places, and occasionally the Oslers used it for longer trips. When the car would not start one day and an important rural consultation was jeopardised, their chauffeur recommended "a young Oxford mechanic by the name of William Morris" who then worked through the night to repair the cracked cylinder head. Morris became the family mechanic and whenever the car would not start, the cry would go up from Osler, "Send for Willy."

In turn Osler became William's physician when he suffered from various ailments. On one occasion, after listening to his medical history, Osler struck Morris a sharp blow in the stomach and told him he had a peptic ulcer which he fully deserved from his lifestyle, saying he was 'bloody lucky' it had not perforated. When Morris told the story, he joked that Osler had also been 'bloody lucky' it did not burst there and then! Morris would also insist that no doctor was worth consulting who did not have Osler's classic book on his shelves, *The Principles and Practice of Medicine*, and he wanted to name a building at the Radcliffe Infirmary after him. It was almost certainly partly in memory of Osler that many of Morris' later medical benefactions were made.

William Osler,
sketched by John Singer Sargent

CHAPTER 4: MOTOR CARS

In 1904 it was estimated that there were 8,500 motor cars on the roads in Britain. By 1910 the figure was about 50,000. By then Morris had developed the mechanical skills necessary to produce cars.

He built new premises in Longwall Street which were described by a local newspaper as 'The Oxford Motor Palace' and changed his business's name from The Oxford Garage to The **Morris Garage** (hence the origin of MG). However, the

Morris (cigarette in mouth) with staff outside Longwall Street workshop in 1907

Longwall Street Garage

building was not large enough and he still needed to take other premises in Queen Street. The site was redeveloped in 1980 and is now used by New College as student accommodation, although the original Longwall Street frontage remains with an exhibition window on the wall recalling the origins of the premises.

By 1911 Morris became convinced that there was going to be high demand for a popularly priced car. He felt sure that what had happened to bicycles would happen with cars, and that the best way to produce them was to do what he had done with bicycles, buying in the separate components from specialist manufacturers, rather than make them all himself. The work would be better, cheaper and less stressful, and the money saved could be used elsewhere.

Although at first he began to sell cars, William had put aside a small area in the garage where he began to design and build his own car. He was hoping to have his first car ready for the 1912 Motor Show in London. Unfortunately it was not, but he had brought up the design plans which met with such approval that he took a substantial number of orders for the car, even before it had appeared – which it duly did the following year.

Morris put a huge amount of effort into that first car and all his employees worked hard alongside him. Alfred Keen recalled the afternoon when the first engine arrived from Coventry and they all worked through the night to put it together. When it was ready William Morris had a short trial trip up the road. One night Elizabeth Tossel, who used to keep Alfred Keen's wife company in the evening while he worked with Morris, was there until about one in the morning. She was about to go home when Morris and Keen came in and said, "Don't go for the moment, we want to show you something." They saw the first Morris car.

When they tested the car she remembered how "they used to keep coming up and down on 'the thing' for days and days… like children playing on a piece of board with four wheels. That's what it looked like." William's father was also thrilled. "I knew Willie could do it," he said, "and Willie did it!" It was called the Morris Oxford, or more affectionately the Bullnose Morris because of its appearance, and it sold for £165 (today about £18,000).

At the turn of the century one English newspaper complained that motor cars were being driven at 60 or 70mph on the unimproved roads of England, and so children were not safe. The Highway Protection League had been founded in 1902 to try to limit the speed of cars and in 1903 the Motor Car Act came into force, introducing new penalties for breaking the speed limit and for reckless driving, with fines and the possibility of jail. The Act also required drivers to hold

The Bullnose Morris

a driving licence, obtained without a test on payment of five shillings, and cars had to display registration plates.

The Automobile Association was founded in 1905 to help motorists avoid police speed traps. By 1906 they had erected thousands of roadside danger and warning signs and remained in charge of road signs until the early 1930s, when they were passed over to local councils. In the year before Morris produced his first car there was still debate as to the benefit of the motor car and the *Economist* asked in its columns whether the advent of the motor car had been a good thing or not, suggesting that the nation would perhaps be richer and happier if motor vehicles were banned altogether.

In August 1912 WRM Motors was formed to undertake manufacture of cars and the Earl of Macclesfield took £4,000 of preference shares. Morris and the Earl had met each other

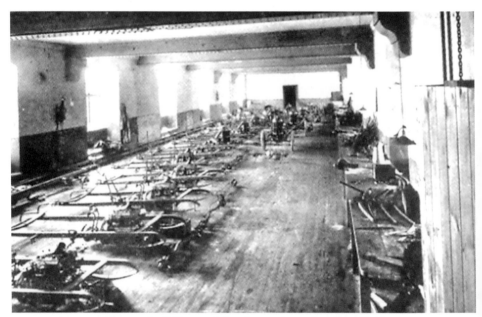

Chassis building at Morris works at Cowley, 1913

previously, when on one occasion as an undergraduate, Macclesfield's car collided with one of Morris' hire cars which was being driven badly with three people in it. Macclesfield threatened to sue Morris who replied, "Don't do that, Sir, or you'll have three expert witnesses against you!" "Who?" he asked. "The Chief Constables of Oxfordshire, Buckinghamshire and Berkshire," was the reply.

By 1914 WRM Motors had produced 1,000 cars. They were reliable, of high quality and sold at an affordable price for many people. Morris had soon outgrown the Longwall Garage and bought a disused Military Training College in Cowley where he began the first mass production line for the construction of motor cars, based on what Ford had been doing in the United States.

Despite having Macclesfield as an early backer, Morris' determination to do things his own way and his unhappy

Coach building at Morris works at Cowley, 1913

29

experience with an earlier partnership led eventually to this relationship being dissolved, even though it lasted into the 1920s. During those years Macclesfield would invite Morris and his team over to his estate, where Morris would take part in cricket or football matches. Macclesfield christened the Morris workers the 'sparking plugs'.

Morris would also attend his work social evenings, often as an active participant, and after one such gathering in an Oxford college there were complaints that people had been kept awake by singing, subsequently to discover that William Morris had been one of the ringleaders.

Until 1913 all the trams in Oxford were drawn by horses and their speed was often exceeded by pedestrians who could not spare the time to ride. Furthermore, the trams often became derailed. In 1902 there was a move to replace the horses with

Postcard showing horse-drawn trams in Oxford

electric trams, but ten years passed and the situation remained unchanged. In November of that year Morris decided to take things into his own hands and provide a motorised bus service in Oxford. He wrote to the city council for a licence to run buses, but the council were unable to come to a decision and did not answer his letter. After waiting three weeks and taking legal advice, Morris decided to provide the service without permission and set up the Oxford Motor Bus company. Daimler of Coventry supplied six buses which were driven to the outskirts of Oxford and the following morning they entered the city and took up their positions at the main horse tram terminal, much to the delight of those making their way to work. It was illegal for the buses to ask for fares, but this was overcome by the sale of coupons at various shops along the route. These coupons resembled bus tickets and entitled the holder to ride on the vehicles.

It was an unqualified success and the public enthusiastically supported the Morris fleet. A compromise was eventually reached, with the council granting twelve licences to Morris without excluding the horse-drawn trams. After a while Morris concluded an agreement with the tramways company, by which they were able to take over his interests and provide a complete bus service in place of their obsolete trams. Morris was recognised as a man who got things done.

In 1914 William was still working in the workshops and was never happier than when he had his head under a bonnet, mending cars which others have given up as past repair. Like a doctor he correlated what he saw with the clinical record of each make of car, noting those aspects that led to the need for less maintenance or a better performance.

Mass production at the Cowley plant

After a number of trials the Morris Oxford, or Bullnose Morris, soon established a reputation for reliability. One such was the London to Edinburgh run in May 1914 when six cars competed. They started from London at 9pm on 29th May and planned to arrive at Edinburgh 24 hours later, making the return journey the following Monday. The time schedule called for an unvarying speed of 20mph, and secret controls were established in each direction to check this. When the speedometer of Morris' car broke down north of Grantham, the maintenance of a steady 20mph was dependent on the driver's ability to estimate his speed and his passenger's accuracy to check the passing milestones with a stopwatch. They did so well that the error on completing the journey was less than two minutes. They won a gold medal, as did the other five Morris cars which had functioning speedometers, thus proving the reliability of the Morris car.

In 1914 Morris wanted to make a four-seat version of the car, but the chassis was too short and the 1018 cc engine too small. The British engine supplier, White & Poppe, were unable to supply the volume of units that Morris required, and so he travelled to the United States to look for components. It was to Continental of Detroit, Michigan, that he eventually turned for the supply of 1548 cc engines. He was due to sail back on the *Empress of Ireland* from Quebec City on 29th May 1914 and it was only by chance that his train was delayed, meaning he had to transfer at the last moment to a later sailing. Just after setting sail, the *Empress of Ireland* was involved in a collision in thick fog with a Norwegian ship near the mouth of the St Lawrence River, and sank within 14 minutes with the loss of 1,100 passengers. Only two days before this, Morris had been in Detroit coming down in a lift

The ill-fated Empress of Ireland

and chatting to the lift operator. He asked what would happen if the lift cable broke and was told that was no need to worry as the automatic brakes would come into action. Morris went across the street for a cup of tea and shortly afterwards somebody rushed in and said that the lift had crashed – all seven occupants had been killed!

William had in fact asked his father to come to the United States with him, but his father did not think he would be of much use to his son and declined with the words, "I'll not be much use to you – when I was there Chicago was just a village, now I hear it's a great city!"

Chapter 5: The First World War

In 1914 the First World War broke out. The war was a mixed blessing, for having begun to produce and sell Morris Oxfords in large numbers, the outbreak of hostilities came as a blow to his hopes of expanding car production to new and higher levels, and output remained low although the orders were still coming in. From mid-1915 a new larger car, the two-seater and four-seater Morris Cowley, had been introduced. At 158 guineas it was among the cheapest in its class and had received good publicity in the motoring press.

In order to fund the war effort, in September 1915 Reginald McKenna, the Chancellor of the Exchequer, introduced a tariff of 33% on luxury imports. At first this excluded commercial vehicles, which were needed for war transport. The tax, which became known as the 'McKenna Duties', was initially intended to be temporary, but lasted for 41 years until it was finally removed in 1956. It effectively abolished the cost advantage of bringing parts in from America. To offset the slump in demand for cars, Morris offered his firm for war

Morris Cowley
Tourer. 1915-1926

A week's output of cars at the old Military Academy in Cowley, 1913

work, an offer gratefully received by Lloyd George, the Munitions Minister at the time.

The factory at Cowley was turned over to making mine sinkers, and by 1916 Morris was involved in their mass production. The government had been experimenting with mine sinkers as a new device in mine-laying. The early British mines were poor and drifted from their original position, but mine sinkers prevented the drift. The sinker was attached to the mine by a long length of cable. The line and sinker were thrown into the sea and initially the mine floated on the surface, but as the sinker fell it paid out the cable until a guide suspended from the sinker touched the bottom. The paying-out mechanism was then locked, and the continued descent of the sinker took the mine to a predetermined depth below the surface. It was decided to use such sinkers in the great North Sea minefield which was being planned. Morris said he could make 250 a week, was given the contract, and during the war he manufactured over 50,000.

He also made a variety of other munitions, including hand grenades and Stokes bomb cases. The latter were used towards the end of the war and would hold a three-inch trench mortar and were invented by Sir Wilfred Stokes. In 1918 Morris was awarded the Order of the British Empire (OBE) for his war work, a British order of chivalry established just a year previously by King George V.

On the family side, Morris' younger sister Alice had married Perceval Minns who worked for Morris as one of his hire car drivers. Percival then moved to Scotland as a chauffeur but in 1914 contracted pneumonia and died. Alice Minns moved back to Oxford with two small children to live with her parents. Two years later she also died, leaving her children as orphans. John, who was six years old at the time, was brought up by his father's family, but three-year-old Pansy was left to be looked after by William's sister, Emily Morris. It was not a particularly happy story and she was fostered for a while with a family who wanted to adopt her but were unable to do so. After a year she was sent to boarding school where she would often remain throughout the school holidays. Lilian Morris was responsible for her clothes and William paid her expenses, and later she moved with Emily's family to London. William and Lilian seemed to have adopted an arm's-length approach with relations in difficulties. Even John Minns was never invited to the Morris' home, although his uncle gave him advice and remained fiercely loyal to him – but even then it was at Morris' office where John was always seen.

On New Year's Day 1916, Frederick Morris died at the age of 66. His grandchildren remembered him as a quiet man who

*William Morris
as a young man*

said very little. He was recovering from the 'flu and, returning from work one day, jumped off the bus just short of the bus stop and fell, dying shortly after – although whether from the effects of injuries or influenza was never clear. William Morris' mother outlived her husband for many years, dying in January 1934. She had seen her son's work prosper and, although glad of his affluence, she stayed amongst her neighbours in her little house in Argyll Street.

"Work is still the natural mission of every real man."

(William Morris, 1924)

CHAPTER 6: BETWEEN THE WARS

In many respects Morris had emerged from WWI in good heart. Obtaining components had been difficult during the war, and at one stage he had even contemplated moving his workforce and their families to Australia, having made serious enquiries about chartering a ship. However, despite the effects of the war, he had a large factory, more machinery, a larger and better trained workforce and sound finances. This contrasted with some of his competitors who found themselves heavily committed to war work, but with a plant that did not readily convert back to peacetime production.

Morris had survived the first three years after the war by sticking closely to the principles adopted before the war – namely, a low price, good-quality, and extensive use of sub-contractors. In addition, he was one of the first to realise the advantages of selling a car complete with all the necessary fitments, in contrast to the general practice of selling a basic car body and charging extra for tyres, tools, electric equipment, windscreens and lamps. He made every effort to stop the purchaser having to buy extras after he had bought the car.

He was cautious about over-committing himself and stuck rigidly to his product policy. The Oxford and the Cowley were the sole models offered in these early years, although with some choice of bodywork. Although American cars were cheaper, Morris was the leader on price in the British market.

Once his distribution network was firmly established, Morris came to concentrate more and more on advertising, although he boasted that the Cowley and Oxford sold themselves without a penny spent on promotion. In fact, he attached great importance to promotion, and from 1919 undertook several promotional activities to increase the public image of his cars. He also put great emphasis on an after-sales service that few other manufacturers were prepared to provide. As early as 1916, Morris had produced a repair manual for the Cowley, and during the 1920s the after-sales service expanded as the distribution network grew, for the retailer was usually also the garage owner. At the same time, Morris set up a technical services department to coordinate policies and prices of the various repair depots and also took the unique step of insisting on a standard set of prices for repairs throughout his dealer network.

In 1920 Lord Northcliffe, the proprietor of the *Daily Mail*, arranged to test the reliability of the Morris car in such a way as it would attract maximum publicity and, no doubt, enhance the sale of his papers. In December John Prioleau, his motoring correspondent, took a standard (but at that stage unnamed) British car on an extensive road tour abroad, involving a variety of conditions and some stretches with no road at all. It was planned to demonstrate any weakness in the car's design and construction. For six months he toured France, Italy, Morocco, Algeria, Tunisia and Spain. The car was christened 'Imshi' which was Arabic for 'get on'. It had done 14,000 miles before it set out and covered another 7,000 miles in this journey. Eventually, in 1922, Prioleau's articles were

reprinted in a book entitled *The Adventures of Imshi*, when it was revealed that it was a Morris Oxford two-seater. It undertook its journey without any preparation and carried it through without any major breakdowns – quite an amazing feat even today.

In 1921 Morris took a big gamble and cut his prices on the assumption that he would sell twice the number of cars. The Morris Cowley two-seater was cut by a fifth to £375 and the Morris Oxford to £510. Some thought it would be a disaster for Morris, but the reverse proved to be the case. In 1921 just over 3,000 cars were sold, in 1922 nearly 7,000, and in 1923, 20,000. These price cuts alarmed and confused rival manufacturers. He managed to persuade his suppliers to take their share of the burden, and at Olympia that year his stand was overwhelmed by customers. There was difficulty getting close, and apparently if people got down to look underneath the car, they could not get up for the crowd.

Between 1919 and 1925 Morris built or purchased factories at Abingdon, Birmingham and Swindon, in addition to the Oxford works. Before long he was Britain's largest manufacturer, a position he was to hold almost without interruption until the Second World War. By now he had contracts running with over 200 firms providing various parts. Using the profits from his business, Morris had a policy of buying up many of the operations of his suppliers. In 1923, when they were unwilling to expand production, Morris bought Hotchkiss' Coventry business (which later became

The Abingdon Factory

Morris Engines), increasing their engine output fourfold from 300 to 1,200 units per week. In 1924 EG Wrigley and Company went into receivership after their major client, Angus-Sanderson (another car maker) was undercut by Morris. Morris subsequently bought all the assets and reconstituted the company as Morris Commercial Cars Limited, manufacturing trucks of different sizes, as well as single and double-decker buses. Following the same policy, he bought the manufacturer of SU Carburettors in 1926. His financial policy was to keep short accounts, demanding payment promptly, and paying what he owed at once.

By this time he was exporting a few cars, although less than 1% of the total manufactured, but there is evidence to show that shipments to Australia, New Zealand, South Africa, India, Malaya and Shanghai were being made.

His personal health suffered during this time due to the long hours and stress of his work, and his doctor told him he was exhausted and needed rest. He suggested a health spa in Germany, which Morris was very reluctant to visit just after the war, but eventually he was persuaded to go and returned home physically and mentally restored.

In 1927 the Morris Cowley accounted for approximately 50,000 of total sales of 60,000. Between 1920 and 1924 Morris had attempted to introduce a large six-cylinder F-type Morris, but only fifty were produced and the project was scrapped. Cecil Kimber had been appointed as sales manager with Morris Garages in 1921, and whilst there he developed a range of special bodies for Morris cars, leading in 1928 to the founding of MG as a separate marque specialising in sports cars. Production subsequently moved outside to a factory at Abingdon in 1929 and Kimber became managing director in July 1930.

In 1925 Morris visited the United States again to look at the American manufacturers. He decided that all steel bodies had come to stay and persuaded Edward G. Budd of the Budd Corporation in Philadelphia to enter a joint venture with him, named The Pressed Steel Company. The following year a large factory was constructed at Cowley opposite Morris' own, joined by a connecting bridge and equipped with modern heavy presses. This came into production in 1927.

Morris' plants worked on during the 1926 General Strike, and that year his profits were £1.25m. His wages were higher than average and the trade unions did not start to affect his business until the late 1920s, when unemployed miners began to arrive in Oxford and their politics influenced his workers.

The Morris Minor as a coachbuilt saloon.

Advert for a Morris Minor in Grace's Guide, 1929

In 1927 he bought Wolseley Motors for £750,000 when the firm went bankrupt. The first Morris Minor was produced in 1928, using an 847 cc engine from Wolseley Motors. The Minor was to provide the base for the MG Midgets, the first of which was produced in 1929. This spread into the small car market helped Morris through the economic depression of the 1930s. In 1928 Henry Ford visited the Cowley Motor works, although Morris was not present. He was expecting criticism but Ford commented, "You folks have nothing to learn from us here."

That year William had an operation for appendicitis (he kept his appendix in a pot and it remains on display in Nuffield House) and suffered from occasional painful sciatica but otherwise kept very well. His overall mental and physical health was enhanced by sea cruises which began in the winter of 1927-28 and continued every year during peacetime. He was never seasick on these voyages, which had begun with the idea of developing overseas trade and continued as a means of keeping in touch with overseas branches. During the cruises Morris enjoyed deck tennis, and his talent for this was helped by the fact that he was ambidextrous and could easily swap his racket from one hand to the other.

As the business continued to grow, Morris reluctantly began to delegate control, although most of the decisions still found their way back to him. He spent more time travelling abroad, usually to Australia. His great faith in Australia as a potential industrial country is thought to have been stimulated by a personal encounter during the First World War. One day, returning from Portsmouth with a colleague, there was a heavy snowstorm and by the time they reached Oxford they were frozen. Morris suggested they should go to the Clarendon Hotel to warm up. Here they met an Australian officer and, after learning who Morris was, he expressed surprise that no one in Britain had taken the trouble to go to Australia to make cars. Morris' colleague noted how interested Morris became and thought that this was when he started planning his Australian exports.

In 1929 Morris received a note asking if he would like to play golf with the Prince of Wales, later to become Edward VIII, and from that year onwards the Court Circular recorded regular audiences of Morris and the Prince. In 1930 Morris Commercial fitted out a six-wheel shooting car for the Prince with sleeping quarters, two enormous tanks for a shower and lavatory fittings.

In 1932 the Morrises bought a house at Huntercombe next to the village of Nuffield in Oxfordshire. The golf course was across the road. They moved in the following year after having several additions and alterations completed. The move to Huntercombe helped provide a new interest for his wife,

Nuffield House in Huntercombe

who took on responsibility for the management of the golf clubhouse – which in the beginning was their house – and she was to become a keen golfer herself. She did not cook and so the opportunity to have meals provided for them in the clubhouse, with ready-made company for them both, made a great deal of sense. The club steward was John Cowley, who was said to have been employed because of his name. He had an old Morris and was seen underneath it one day. When his boss asked him what was wrong, he said it was worn out. Morris agreed and the next day a new one was delivered to him, fully taxed and insured. On one occasion Morris returned from London on a slow train by mistake and Cowley came and picked him up at Henley on his Norton motorbike with Morris riding pillion.

For many years there was a popular story that Morris had been refused membership of the golf club as he was a tradesman and so as a solution he bought the club. Although you still hear this story today, it is not true. Indeed, the club had fallen into financial difficulties and Morris, who had been a member for some years, bought the club and gave it to the members.

William Morris was always attracted by broken-down cars. On one occasion while playing golf, he saw a man under a broken-down car. He left the golf course, went over to the car, and solved the problem. As he disappeared into the clubhouse to wash his hands, the car owner commented to the other golfers, "Pretty decent fellow that, seems to know a little bit about the innards of a car."

Soon after the move to Huntercombe, Morris started the practice of going to Australia by ship almost every winter. He would leave in January and return in March. Lilian did not go with him but he was usually accompanied by Wilfred Hobbs or another member of the organisation. While he was away, Lilian Morris was often driven to the south of France by Maule, the chauffeur, accompanied by her sister and brother-in-law.

Lilian was a shy woman and was happiest with her dogs. She did not relish the public arena into which her husband was thrown. She would rarely accompany him to dinners and refused to be introduced to the Prince of Wales, but when on one occasion a visit to a film studio was organised, she was enthusiastic and enjoyed the occasion.

In 1934 William Morris was created a baronet and became Lord Nuffield, taking the name from the village where he was living. His first choice of title was Cowley, but that had already been taken. A baron is the lowest rank in the British peerage, used originally to denote a tenant-in-chief of the early Norman kings who held his lands by the feudal tenure of 'barony' and who was entitled to attend the Great Council, which by the thirteenth century had developed into the Parliament of England. Some years later, Morris was further honoured when he was elevated in the peerage to Viscount.

The first Morris car to be sold for just £100 was in 1931. That year he sold 50,000 but by 1935 Morris Motors was producing 100,000 cars a year, a third of all the cars produced in Britain. By this time he was the major industrialist in the UK and one of the largest in Europe.

As a peer of the realm, William and his wife were invited to the coronation of King George VI which took place on 12th May 1937. He had left it too late to book a hotel room, so instead he and his wife stayed with the superintendent of Guy's Hospital, Sir Herbert Eason. Eason's daughter, who was

15 at the time, recalled that he was drinking champagne and the whole dinner was hilarious. He kept putting the prefix 'eggs' instead of 'ex' in every word he could think of, and, "we ended up parading around in his coronation robes, sword and all." Guy's Hospital took care to court him in a way that Oxford University seemed not to have learned. In due course he became the largest benefactor to Guy's Hospital since their original founder, Thomas Guy. To this day a statue of Morris stands in the main courtyard of Guy's Hospital.

Kidnap Attempt

On the 25th May 1938 there was an attempt to kidnap Lord Nuffield. It was an elaborate plot by an experienced blackmailer, John Thornton, who was later arrested by armed police at the Cowley car works. He had hatched a plot to imprison Nuffield on a yacht off the Suffolk coast and raid his bank account. Once on board, Nuffield would have been forced to write three letters – one to his secretary, saying he would be away for a week; a second to his bank, saying money could be withdrawn from his account by a Dr Webb; and the third identifying Thornton as Dr Webb. Thornton recruited an old friend, Major Arthur Ramsden, who was to keep Nuffield chained on the yacht while he collected the money, but Ramsden was taken aback when he heard of the plot and went straight to the police. Thornton was jailed for seven years for possessing automatic pistols and ammunition, and for conspiring to kidnap Nuffield.

The millionth car rolled off the works on 22nd May 1939. Nuffield marked the occasion by buying it himself and presenting it to the Ladies' Association of Guy's Hospital, whose appeal fund benefited by nearly £1,700 from a special draw in which the car was offered as a prize. That year Morris was delighted to be elected as a Fellow of the Royal Society for his support of universities and science.

"I've lived long enough to know that it is not always the men who have an expensive education who do things."

(William Morris, 1929)

CHAPTER 7: THE SECOND WORLD WAR

From the beginning of the Second World War widespread bombing had been expected and Lilian Morris herself was terrified of a German invasion. She was suffering from a goitre of the thyroid gland and her doctor advised that she should go away for a break. Morris discussed matters with Robert Macintosh, an anaesthetist and medical friend, asking if he would take her to the United States. He agreed and they sailed on the American liner *Washington* with a large American flag painted on the side with the intention of discouraging U-boat attacks. It is unclear how long Lilian was there, but an entry in her diary in 1943 recorded, 'Went to Buckingham Palace. Talked with the Queen, King, and two Princesses.'

The motor industry formed one of the biggest reserves on which Britain could draw when war came, and one which was also quickly available because normal production could be suspended and its engineering resources and skills turned over to a wide variety of munitions production.

During the 1930s Nuffield had taken an increasing role as a man of national importance and was very concerned about the war preparations going on in Germany. He tried to persuade a hesitant British Government to start preparing for war. He offered the Minister of Air a proposal in which he would supply and build aero engines for the Supermarine Spitfire. Although ordered by the Air Ministry in 1936, not a single plane had been built, and so a new factory at Castle Bromwich was obtained by the Air Secretary and Nuffield was placed in charge. He had claimed he could produce 50 Spitfires a week but by May 1940, at the height of the Battle of France, for reasons that are not clear, not one Spitfire had been built. That month Lord Beaverbrook was placed in charge of all aircraft production, Nuffield was sacked, and from 1941 the plant handed over to Vickers, Supermarine's parent company.

Much of the Cowley plant, however, was turned over to aircraft repair and from 1940 the plant built forty Tiger Moths per week – these were the training aircraft for the Royal Air Force. Cowley became the headquarters for the whole Civilian Repair Organisation (CRO) for the Royal Air Force. They were initially hesitant about allowing civilians to do the repairs, but their disquiet was quelled when they heard that Nuffield was going to be in charge. The headquarters of the CRO was initially at Cowley but then in early 1940 it was moved to Merton College to reduce the risk of air attack. Nuffield's brief was to salvage everything, and his comment was, "It looks as if our work is to mend everything except broken hearts."

By the time of the Dunkirk evacuation, Cowley was repairing twelve aircraft a week. During the three crucial months of the Battle of Britain, it returned 150 seriously damaged aircraft to the air, as well as acting as an accident and emergency department for fighter pilots who landed their Spitfires and Hurricanes on the newly constructed airfield at the Cowley works. During the Battle of Britain, one tired pilot in a white sweater was greeted with, "You were here the day before yesterday!" and he replied, "Yes and I have done eight sorties this morning." He promptly fell asleep before he could

Cowley Morris Motors airfield, in 1941 and 1947

tell the foreman what had happened. The same pilot landed again the next day to the comment, "This is getting to be a habit, my boy!"

Of the total number of aircraft issued to the fighter squadrons during the Battle of Britain, 35% were repaired and only 65% were new. In November 1943, 63,600 workers were employed at the Cowley works while, overall, four million were employed on new airframe production over the whole period of the war. The CRO repaired and put back into service 75,000 aircraft and it was said that Nuffield rebuilt the RAF several times over. Its crucial achievement was during the Battle of Britain when the repair units added critical weight to the scale of fighting strength on the Allied side.

No. 50 MAINTENANCE UNIT, R.A.F.

MORRIS WORKS
COWLEY, OXFORD

APPENDIX "A".

Part 4.   ATTACHMENT TO OPERATIONS RECORD - APRIL.
             SALVAGE UNITS.

Crash inspections carried out during month. 171
Aircraft Provisionally serviceable. ....
    repairable by Unit, Cat. "A"   8
    repairable by Contractors on site.   96
    repairable at Works   31
    Category   ....
    Enemy - salved.
    Inspected and reported to 43 Group.   ___
                          TOTAL -   171
Airframes or Fuselages
    Transferred to Contractors for recovery of   22
                                    spares.   11

Airframes - Instructions   3
German Aircraft salved   38
Obstructions dealt with   28

55

The first Nuffield prototype tank from 1937

Several British officers who attended the Russian autumn manoeuvres in 1936 were impressed by the fast light tanks which the Red Army were using, and the War Office asked Nuffield to assist in developing a similar speedy vehicle for the British Army. One limitation to their speed had been their suspension, potentially knocking the driver unconscious when driving over certain obstacles. The Russian tanks had much better suspension and a system designed by an American engineer was incorporated into Nuffield tanks so that the tank was capable of 30mph without serious maintenance problems.

Outside Oxford the Nuffield factories made over 200 Cruiser tanks and then 300 of their successor, the Crusader. Forty of the first Nuffield cruiser tanks were in the British Expeditionary Force in France and were able to surround Dunkirk and ease the rescue of over 300,000 men from the beaches.

The Cruiser Tank Mark 3, A13, which benefitted from Morris' design work

Nuffield also flew two bomber-loads of technicians to North Africa to modify 750 Crusader tanks for the 8th Army before the battle of El Alamein. In addition to all this, he was producing Bren gun carriers, glider parts in preparation for D-Day landings, midget submarines, torpedoes and mine sinkers. He made Bofors anti-aircraft guns, designed in the 1930s by the Swedish arms manufacturer AB Bofors, and Oxford vapourisers delivering a given concentration of a volatile anaesthetic agent for use under battle conditions.

CHAPTER 8: POST-WAR CONSOLIDATION

After the war there was an inevitable period of readjustment to the conditions of peace, which on the one hand produced a heavy demand for any kind of vehicle, but on the other production was impeded by rationing, especially of steel. Nevertheless, car production restarted, with the pre-war Morris Eight (horsepower) and Ten designs. In 1948 the Eight was replaced by what is probably the most famous Morris car, the Morris Minor, designed by Alec Issigonis (who later went on to design the Mini). The Morris Ten was replaced by a new 1948 Morris Oxford MO, styled like a larger version of the Minor. A later Morris Oxford (the 1956 Morris Oxford III) was the basis for the design of India's Hindustan Ambassador, which was the iconic car in India and continued in production until 2014.

Nuffield now kept himself in the background. He was in his late sixties and unable to play the full role that he wanted to, but was determined that his organisation should play a leading part in bringing the country

The classic Morris Minor shape

59

The 1948 advertisement for the Morris Minor and the Morris Oxford

back to prosperity, to combat the American challenge, and to develop international markets. He took some practical steps to set up plants abroad – first of all in Australia – and then he looked at the possibility of India and South Africa (and less successfully in the United States). It gave the signal that the British car corporations were in a position to compete on the global stage.

Morris was very fond of Australia and saw enormous potential there, making a total of 22 trips by boat over many years. He had decided that his company should make a completely Australian car and the first step was to make the bodies locally. In 1945, on a visit there, he formed Nuffield (Australia) Propriety Ltd and a site was chosen on the Victoria Park Race Course in Sydney, with arrangements to buy it from the Victoria Park Club.

Although the park was no longer used for horse-racing and the Sydney Turf Club's lease on the land ran out in 1947, the Club had been established by the state government to promote horse-racing. This gave the state government special powers over a number of designated race courses, including Victoria Park, although they needed top-level approval to restart racing.

An appeal was made to the premier of New South Wales for a ruling as to whether such a resumption would be allowed. Despite urgent appeals, no definitive answer had been received when Morris arrived in Australia early in 1946. He then decided that the Sydney project had waited long enough, and arranged a contract with Richard Industries Ltd of Adelaide to carry out all the Morris car body-building work in Australia. He was then accused of breaking faith with Sydney, which forced him to publish the whole

Aerial view of Nuffield (Australia) Pty at Victoria Park

correspondence that his managing director had had with the Premier's office. All this led to an enormous political storm and suggestions were made that the Premier had a vested interested in the Turf Club which had in fact been created by his company. There was considerable local feeling against the Turf Club and the alleged apathy of the government which had caused the one-million-pound company to be lost to South Australia. Very quickly it was announced that the Turf Club did not intend to resume racing and that the government would offer every assistance to Morris, although this came too late to prevent the contract with Richard Industries in Adelaide. However, on his next visit to Australia in 1948, Morris did announce several plans for a factory on the Victoria Park Race Course and work was put in hand for making car bodies, gear boxes and engines, the site eventually becoming the assembly factory for Austin Motors as well as Morris Motors. Australia was to honour Morris with three honorary degrees from the Universities of Sydney, Melbourne and New South Wales.

With the fear of American competition and also to secure the future of Morris Motors before his death, Morris sanctioned negotiations with Austin's chairman, Leonard Lord, to merge both companies. In 1952 the British Motor Corporation (BMC) was formed. Morris was Chairman for its first year and was then succeeded by Lord, with Morris, now 75, taking the title of Honorary President. He would still attend his office regularly and offer advice to his colleagues. Two years later in 1954 he finally retired for good, leaving the huge firm he had built up so assiduously since 1913 to be run completely by others.

BMC (Australia) car identity plate, and a BMC Service and Sales sign

Chapter 9: Morris' Benefactions

In his lifetime, Morris gave thirty million pounds (£1.4 billion in today's money) to charity, largely in two major areas: health and education. He once said it was the easiest thing in the world to make money, but it's damned difficult to know how to get rid of it!

Amongst his earliest benefactions were £10,000 (£518,000) in 1926 to enable parents to visit their children who were in borstals. In the same year he gave the University of Oxford £10,000 (£518,000) to establish the King Alfonso XIII Chair of Spanish Studies. He had become extremely interested in the possibility of business in Spain and South America and had realised the very limited provision of Spanish studies in Great Britain. Again, amongst his earlier donations were gifts to Coventry and Warwickshire Hospital and to the Birmingham General Hospital in 1927. The Oxford Hospitals benefited even more from 1930 onwards, for these were all in districts where his factories were located and where he had a particular interest in the welfare of his people.

Nuffield had been very generous in the provision of club rooms, sports facilities, the provision of dental and medical services, and he made a major effort to employ seriously disabled people. In fact, in the early 1950s there were 700 disabled people working for the Nuffield organisation, and in this he was years ahead of his time. He also provided a unique benefaction for his employees and put aside over two million pounds' (£114 million) worth of shares in the mid-1930s to give his employees an interest in the profits of the organisation.

In the 1930s during the depression, he set up a trust for the 'Special Areas' with a capital of two million pounds (£113 million). 'Special Areas' was the term he applied to avoid the pessimism associated with the name 'depressed areas'. The trust was designed to help regions that had high unemployment by providing financial support for businesses that were going under, or needed support to get started. In the years the trust was active, it paid out nearly two-and-a-half million pounds (£143 million), but ten years later the trust had just as much money available. This was due to the fact that most of the businesses that had started up with the Nuffield Trust's help had repaid the money they had been given, which was then transferred to the King Edward Hospital Fund, yet another fund established by Nuffield.

A typical example of the Special Areas Trust Fund was the Whitehaven Collieries which employed 2,500 men. The colliery closed in 1935, and since it had been the main source of employment in the town the effect was devastating. However, in 1937 the Nuffield Trust provided finances which enabled the Coltness Iron Company Ltd to take over the White Haven Collieries and reopen and redevelop them. Eventually full production at the collieries was restored and the situation in White Haven was transformed. Nuffield was awarded the Freedom of White Haven in 1953, and when he went to receive the award, virtually the whole town turned out to welcome him. He had last seen the town when most of the shops were closed, unemployed men were standing at the street corners and many young boys were leaving school had no chance of a job.

Nuffield's medical benefactions were enormous. He played golf mostly on Saturdays and Sundays which brought him into the company of different groups of people and a ready-made set of acquaintances. Many of them were consultant doctors in London and the contacts he made led to many of the most important benefactions he was to make.

The principal set was a group of doctors from Guy's Hospital in London, including Robert Macintosh, one of Morris' very few close friends. He was a New Zealander who had come to Britain in December 1915 and served in the Royal Flying Corps. He was shot down behind enemy lines in 1917 and taken prisoner, escaping several times. After the war, Macintosh trained at Guy's Hospital Medical School, qualifying in 1924, and was then preparing for a career as a surgeon, during which time he earned a living by giving dental anaesthetics. This led to his interest in anaesthesia. He said of Morris:

He never did any reading. I have never known him read a book in his whole life, and when it came to the papers, it was only the front-page news. Figures though, that was the extraordinary thing, he could read a balance sheet which completely baffled me.

And talking of his golfing interest he said:

He played golf, but barely waited for the ball to be put on the tee, and many thought one day he would get his caddie's hand rather than the ball. He was apt to forget his backstroke, paid little attention, did not address the ball correctly, and never played a full round. After a few holes he would often say, 'Come in and have a cup of tea', and I've known him then go over and repair my car!

Nuffield was always interested in medical complaints, both his own and other people's, and was a great taker of pills. He had milk of magnesia delivered on a silver tray at 3:30pm in the afternoon. Indeed, at his office in Cowley he had a cupboard full of different medicines, as well as a boomerang and map of Australia on the wall. Macintosh denied the rumour that Morris, as a child, had wanted to become a surgeon, but his gifts and legacies would give him a vicarious involvement in medicine. On one occasion Sir John Stallworthy, the eminent gynaecologist, was asked to examine his sister, Mrs Yockney, but was told by Morris that she could not be operated on as she had a bad heart. Stallworthy replied that unless the tumour was dealt with she was far more likely to die of that. Morris then told Stallworthy to remove her appendix as well, at which point Stallworthy had had enough and told Morris that he would either operate his way or not at all, to which Morris replied, "Terms accepted."

His gifts to the Medical School at Oxford University and the Oxford hospitals were phenomenal. Starting in 1930 he purchased the Radcliffe Observatory building for £100,000, together with some grounds which were due to be vacated when the Observatory was transferred to the clear skies of South Africa. This enlarged the neighbouring Radcliffe Infirmary, which Macintosh described as "a poor little country hospital". Although there was a distinguished Preclinical Medical School in

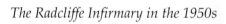

The Radcliffe Infirmary in the 1950s

The Radcliffe Observatory

Oxford, students went to London, Liverpool or Birmingham for their clinical studies, and many patients would travel to London for surgical operations.

The Observatory buildings were unsuitable for hospital purposes, but Nuffield was looking forward to the development of Oxford as a Postgraduate Centre for Medical Research, and in 1935 he gave further money to establish the Nuffield Institute of Medical Research, in the Observatory.

He also provided money to build a Maternity Home at the Radcliffe Infirmary in 1932, together with an additional wing in 1937. The Wingfield Orthopaedic Hospital (now the Nuffield Orthopaedic Centre) in Headington received numerous gifts from him, sufficient to allow it to be rebuilt – it was then known as the Wingfield-Morris Hospital. He had close connections with the famous orthopaedic surgeon, Gathorne Girdlestone, who later was to become the first Nuffield Professor of

The Fielden Ward at the renovated Wingfield-Morris hospital in Headington

Orthopaedics. One of their first meetings was in 1925 when Girdlestone was at dinner. There was a knock on the door, and the maid said that a badly dressed man was asking for him. Girdlestone assumed this to be a workman. He went to the door where Morris stood saying, "I understand your hospital is hard up and you need £1,000 to keep going. Perhaps you would accept this," and handed him a cheque. At a later stage he gave £150,000 to the Orthopaedic Hospital after his wife had been treated there for rheumatism under Girdlestone.

However, it was in 1936 that he made his major gift to the Medical School. He had numerous discussions over a project to develop a Postgraduate Medical Centre of Excellence in Oxford with Sir Farquhar Buzzard, the Regius Professor of Medicine. Buzzard had been stimulated by the young Hugh Cairns, a former Rhodes Scholar from Australia and at this time a consultant surgeon at the London Hospital. Cairns was eventually to become the first Nuffield Professor of Surgery. Buzzard had succeeded Sir Archibald Garrod as Regius Professor of Medicine, and he in turn had succeeded Sir William Osler, whom Nuffield knew well – it was that association with Osler which may have stimulated Nuffield's medical philanthropy.

In 1936 it was Buzzard's turn to become President of the British Medical Association and the annual banquet was held in Oxford. Buzzard invited Nuffield to be the guest of honour. In his speech Buzzard talked of an ambitious dream for a School of Clinical Medicine at Oxford, and afterwards slipped a copy of Cairns' proposal into Nuffield's pocket saying, "Read this when you get home." Cairns had already spoken to Nuffield and Nuffield told him that he was 'a man with fire in his belly', and that he would back the scheme.

Nuffield with Hugh Cairns, the first Nuffield Professor of Surgery

Lord Nuffield donates an unknown amount to a nurses' collection...
... but later it proved to be a cheque for £100,000!

However, then came a typical Nuffield twist. Initially three professors were planned – medicine, surgery, obstetrics and gynaecology. Nuffield insisted on a fourth, a professor of anaesthetics. There were no professors of anaesthetics in the British Empire, and Oxford did not regard it as a subject of sufficient standing or merit, arguing that any competent doctor should be able to give an anaesthetic. Nuffield disagreed, founded on his personal experience as a young man when he had all his bad teeth removed. The nitrous oxide given by the local dentist did not last very long, Morris had horrible nightmares and remembered the feeling of suffocation. He contrasted it with another operation where Macintosh was the anaesthetist, when he regained consciousness demanding to know when the operation was about to start, after it had already finished!

Nuffield assumed that his request, or rather demand, for a fourth chair in anaesthetics would be automatically accepted, and so he was surprised when Buzzard called on him at home one Sunday afternoon to tell him that deeply grateful as the university was, a chair in anaesthetics would expose both the university and Nuffield to ridicule. Nuffield thanked Buzzard in a friendly way for pointing this out and Buzzard left, assuming that Nuffield had agreed to drop the anaesthetic chair. Two weeks went by, after which Buzzard telephoned to enquire when the university could announce its medical benefaction, only to be told by Nuffield that at the last interview he had understood that the university had declined the offer. It then became crystal-clear that his offer was for four chairs or none. The university gave in, but Nuffield had not finished, and insisted on Macintosh being nominated for that chair. Macintosh was taken by surprise – he had a thriving private practice in London and saw little attraction to transferring to academic life in Oxford. However, he did not want to cause a breach between his medical friends and Nuffield, and so it was agreed that he could move to Oxford but keep his practice in London.

Nuffield offered the university one-and-a-quarter million pounds for the endowment of a Medical School Trust. Shortly afterwards the congregation of the university was called to accept the gift and express the gratitude of the university. The Chancellor, Lord Halifax, was there, and it was during that meeting (after the gift had been announced) that, quite out of turn, Nuffield stood up and asked if he might say something. He announced that he decided that one-and-a-quarter million pounds was perhaps not quite enough, and he had decided to increase his donation to two million pounds. That is, in today's money, at least 114 million pounds! This allowed the Chairs of Surgery, Clinical Medicine, Orthopaedic Surgery, Anaesthetics, and Obstetrics and Gynaecology to be established, and undoubtedly was the beginning of the modern Medical School at Oxford as we know it today. Nuffield expressed his desire for the future of Oxford medicine in the following way:

All I want is for the Medical School to turn out twenty brilliant men a year who would go out and teach others.

He later provided a further £200,000 (£11.4m) to provide additional buildings at the hospital for the use of the Medical School, and this primarily went to build additional wards for the Professor of Surgery and the Professor of Obstetrics and Gynaecology. He also provided a further £300,000

(£17,160,000) to provide a fund to ensure that adequate facilities could be provided for the Clinical School as a whole, including non-university staff, as was befitting a major postgraduate centre.

Nuffield's aim, of course, was to provide the wherewithal to establish an outstanding postgraduate medical centre, and not just an undergraduate medical school. He did not want his professors and their staff burdened by having to teach undergraduates. During the war, clinical students were evacuated from London and large numbers came to Oxford. After the war it was decided that Oxford should continue to have a postgraduate medical school as well as an under-graduate one, and his dream of a postgraduate medical school, second-to-none, came to fruition. Fifty years after his death in one international analysis of medical schools, the Oxford Medical School was ranked the top medical school in the world, illustrating the effect Nuffield's benefaction has had on medicine in Oxford.

One Saturday in 1939 Professor Howard Florey called on Nuffield to ask for £3,000 to complete some interesting work on a penicillin mould. "Is that enough?" asked Nuffield. "I think so," replied Florey. "If that is all you want you shall have it," came the reply. He helped again in 1942 and made a substantial grant to support the funding provided by the Medical Research Council for penicillin research. In 1948, because of the work on penicillin, Nuffield endowed three research fellowships at Lincoln College and three members of the penicillin team were elected to these – Norman Heatley, Edward Abraham and Gordon Sanders.

In 1938 Morris established a Dominion Scholarship Fund with £170,000. He had always had a close personal interest in

Norman Heatley working at the laboratory bench c. 1940

the Dominions and this provided scholarships for young medical men from universities in Australia, New Zealand and South Africa to come to England for postgraduate training. From time to time, further gifts were given to the Oxford hospitals and the Medical School to help with specific problems.

He also made large gifts in 1938 to St Thomas's Hospital (£100,000 – £5.4 million today) and Guy's Hospital, via the consultants whom he had met at Huntercombe Golf Club. He provided Guy's with money to build a new private wing in 1935, Nuffield House, with a donation of £73,000, and then in 1936 he provided a further £80,000 for a much-needed extension to the Nurse's Home. On one occasion when he made a large donation to Guy's, he announced it at a lunch given at the hospital. Afterwards a friend congratulated him on his gift and he replied, "Yes, and do you know I did not know I was going to do it until I got up."

His direct personal gifts to Guy's Hospital totalled some £170,000 (£9,194,000) and he later became a member of the Board of Governors, and finally Honorary President of the Hospital. It is interesting that there is a full-sized statue of Nuffield in the forecourt of Guy's Hospital by Maurice Lambert, but to our knowledge there is not a single statue of

Nuffield in Oxford where he had made so many contributions – although he was given the freedom of the City of Oxford in 1951. In 1958, at the Queen's invitation, he was made a Companion of Honour, the most prestigious of honours awarded by the Queen and restricted to only 65 living members.

Nuffield's interest in the training of doctors was shown again by a large benefaction of £250,000 (£7,268,000) to the Royal College of Surgeons of England in 1948, providing a residential centre for young surgeons who came to the college for study and research, as well as scientific laboratories. This was the Nuffield College of Surgical Sciences, and the work in its laboratories produced several Fellows of the Royal Society and one Nobel Prize-winner. In 1949 Nuffield was made an Honorary Fellow of the college.

Numerous other specific benefactions were made for medical purposes, particularly for disabled children and adults, where over a large number of years he gave large sums of money for this purpose and, indeed, over £200,000 (£5,814,000) was given in Australia and New Zealand for the help of disabled people.

On one occasion he walked into a social services department wearing an old raincoat and asking questions about helping old people. He was about to be shown the door when he said, "It seems as if you are on the right lines, I'll give you £50,000 for a pilot project."

In 1938 he visited an anaesthetic department in London and was shown the 'Both' Portable Cabinet Respirator for maintaining respiration in patients, most of whom had polio. More commonly known as the 'iron lung', it was a negative pressure ventilator invented in 1937 by Both, an Australian

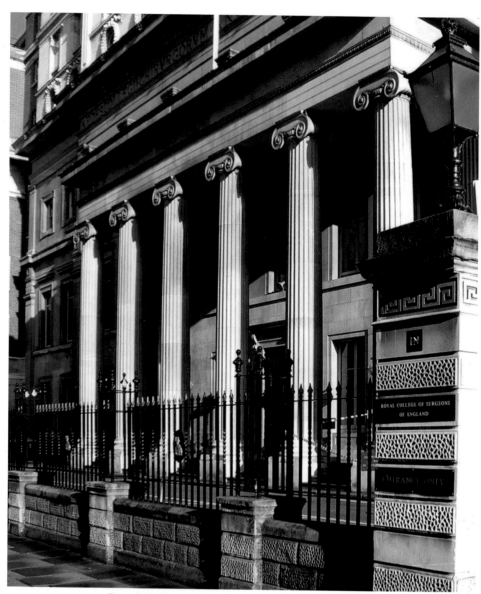

Royal College of Surgeons in Lincoln's Inn Fields

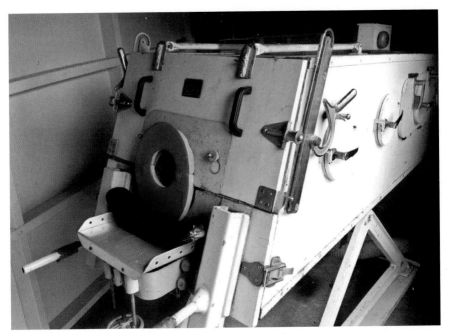

The Both 'Iron Lung'

engineer. Made from plywood rather than metal, these were still experimental and very few were available. Nuffield planned to have 5,000 constructed in his factory in Oxford. Although the war eventually stopped their production, some 1,700 were completed and distributed in Great Britain and the Commonwealth.

In 1939 Morris founded The Nuffield Trust for the Forces of the Crown after writing to the then Secretary of State for War:

> *I am anxious to make some personal contribution towards the comfort and well-being of those who are giving up their home surroundings in the service of our country. For this purpose, I intend to place in the hands of trustees one million shares in Morris Motors, of a present value of approximately £1.5 million, yielding today an income of*

some £105,000 per annum to be devoted towards improving the facilities for the Forces, at the discretion of the trustees. I intend this gift to be a permanent memorial to the spirit which animates us today.

It helped to fill the gap between what was provided from official sources and those other elements which made living conditions more comfortable, or recreation more enjoyable, for those serving in the Second World War (or the numerous operational deployments that have followed).

Nuffeld became interested in provident funds, which provided a form of medical insurance for those who wanted private care. Eventually this became a national scheme with all the provident associations united, becoming the British United Provident Association (or BUPA) which was underwritten by one of Nuffield's funds. The Nuffield Hospital Provincial Trust was another large trust which he endowed with a million pounds (£34 million) to try and spread the distribution of medical facilities throughout the country. In a letter to Walter Elliott, Minister of Health, eight years before the National Health Insurance Act appeared on the statute books, he wrote:

It is my hope that a truly national hospital service may evolve which will embrace all that is best of both public and voluntary effort with the maximum economy to the State and to the private purse.

Much of the plans behind the trust were adopted by the National Health Service when it was introduced in 1948.

Nuffield College

Nuffield had often thought that he would like to establish a college within the university which would specialise in applied engineering. He presented this proposal to the Vice Chancellor who was delighted with the offer but did not feel that engineering was appropriate for Oxford. Part of the reason for this was that the university did not want to step on Cambridge's toes as the two universities had an informal agreement that they would not duplicate each other's special activities. Nuffield was persuaded that what was needed was a college at a postgraduate level devoted to research in social studies. Reluctantly, Nuffield agreed with these suggestions and in 1937 provided £1,000,000 (£55 million) plus the land for the new Nuffield College, which was to be built on the old canal wharf site. The college was awarded its charter in 1958.

Morris also gave the university £100,000 (£5,553,000) for a new Physical Chemical Laboratory, and was the person responsible for rescuing St Peter's Hall from certain closure. St Peter's Hall, now called St Peter's College, was founded by Bishop Frances Chavasse and his son Christopher Chavasse, but in 1933 the worldwide financial crisis had struck down the Hall's principal supporter, an educational trust, which had guaranteed the £70,000 mortgage secured on the Hall's own buildings. Nuffield's involvement came after the Rev Christopher Chavasse had had several long discussions with him, a connection probably linked to the fact that Chavasse was the also the Rector of St Aldate's Church which Morris' mother attended. Today the college continues to commemorate Morris along with three members of the Chavasse family: Frances who became the first Bishop of Liverpool, Christopher, who became the first Master, and his

Nuffield College, Oxford

St Peter's College, Oxford

brother Noel, a doctor, who died of wounds in the First World War but was one of the few people to receive a bar to his Victoria Cross.

The Nuffield Foundation

The last and greatest of Lord Nuffield's major trusts endowed by him consisted of shares worth £10,000,000 (£402 million) and was founded in 1943. Its purpose was to advance health and the prevention and relief of sickness by medical research and teaching, the advancement of social well-being, the care and comfort of the aged and poor, and the advancement of education. The Foundation's grants and support of institutions has been spread not only through the United Kingdom but throughout the Commonwealth. The Nuffield Foundation was for some time the largest philanthropic trust in the country, worth approximately £30 million in the 1950s (equivalent to about £1.8 billion today). This was reflected in the scope of some of the early projects funded, including those in medical genetics, physics and health. For example, the Foundation funded the work of two scientists who later became Nobel Prize-winners – Patrick Blackett's investigation of cosmic rays, and Dorothy Hodgkin's research on the structure of penicillin, vitamin B12 and insulin.

Throughout the 1950s, the Foundation was also a major funder of the Lovell Telescope at Jodrell Bank Observatory. In a rare personal intervention, following the success of the telescope in transmitting signals to the American Pioneer V deep space probe, Lord Nuffield matched the Foundation's final grant to the project with a personal donation.

Lovell Telescope at Jodrell Bank Observatory

CHAPTER 10: NUFFIELD THE MAN

Nuffield was a shy but very determined and polite man with a brilliant brain, and in his younger days he sported a dark trim dynamic figure flowing with physical energy. Full of restless energy when sitting, he would put one leg over the other, then within a few minutes fling his legs across the arm of the chair. After a few minutes he would jump up and walk a few steps back and forth. He was often seen on the factory floor walking and talking with his staff and in the early days would know them all by name. Those who did know him well could tell whether he was in a good or bad mood when visiting them. The further his hat was back on his head, the worse temper he was in!

He believed in leading, not driving, his workers and allowed smoking in his works – except in those areas where there was a special risk of fire. This was in contrast to the United States where smoking was banned in all automobile factories. He argued that the fire danger was less if the men smoked openly than if they hurriedly put cigarettes down when the foreman came round.

The chief characteristic that he looked for in his managers was loyalty. It took a while for them to get to know him and read his mind. Once, when management plans were put forward and a new man asked some questions about important details, it was

Nuffield with one of his beloved cars

clear to those who knew Nuffield that they had his consent. The new man asked tentatively if he would let him know as soon as he had made his decision, so they could make an early start. Nuffield looked at his watch and replied, "It's five to twelve. If you want to make a quick start you can start at 12 o'clock."

Miss Ena Berry, his secretary from 1939, said Morris never read a letter nor dictated a reply. He wanted to hear the meat of it and then just indicated the type of reply he wanted. It put a heavy responsibility on his private secretaries.

Relationships between Morris and Oxford University were always fraught. There was a mixture of both respect and disdain on the side of the university, and John Betjeman, who was later to become the Poet Laureate, put his finger on this difficult relationship in his book *An Oxford University Chest*:

It has always occurred to me that the great black wall of

the university has shadowed his life. He has stormed it and won. Oxford is no longer primarily a university town but primarily an industrial town. The shade of the wall may now seem grateful to Lord Nuffield. He is able to bolster its crumbling bastions, to mortice it with gold.

On 2nd December 1936, a *Punch* cartoon entitled the 'Horn of Plenty' by EH Shepard (the illustrator of Winnie-the-Pooh) showed Morris pouring a stream of coins into begging bowls thrust out by beaming academics.

On the other hand, one former registrar of the university said after Nuffield's death,

He never was at his ease and his presence imposed constraints on the other members of the common room. Most would be anxious to make a good impression so that free and forthright conversation was impossible.

It was the same at the golf club when he often boasted that he had never paid more than £5 for any of his suits and asked the doctors what was wrong with them. Macintosh comments that, "We could have told him, but no one liked to contradict him, and silence was converted to approval!"

On one occasion, leaving Balliol college after dinner, he was handed his hat and coat, looked twice at the hat he was given and asked, "Is that my hat?" To which the porter replied, "That I cannot say, Sir, but it's the one you gave me when you came in."

Little is known or written of the Morris marriage. Both partners were very protective of each other and no interviews were permitted with Mrs Morris (Lady Nuffield). Being married to a man who is wedded to his business is never an easy situation. Mrs Macintosh, a close friend of Lilian, said Lady Nuffield had made her mind up not to have children because she had a horror and fear of childbirth. William Morris was not good with children, but later in their marriage Lilian used to take over the skating rink in Oxford at Christmas to give children's parties, which had nothing to do with her husband's works, and she enjoyed distributing presents. Whilst she had a retiring nature and shunned public life, she was in fact a skilful motorist, and when driving her husband, was able to do so without him commenting adversely on her driving.

Childlessness was something that appeared to be a great sadness in Morris' mind and he once said, "I have more than any man can want, and a title, but all this dies when I die. This is my personal tragedy."

Morris was always a hands-on man. At his home he had had cupboards installed in his bedroom which opened out to reveal a built-in workshop complete with a bench vice and a range of tools. When he had difficulty sleeping he would repair clocks, mend cigarette lighters or shoes, or do some other odd job to keep him occupied during the night. However, when he wanted a brazier in the room his wife put her foot down! He also had an interest in meteorology and possessed three barometers, a hygrometer, thermometer and a wind direction indicator. Amongst his relatively few books were a dictionary, an introduction to pharmacy, and *The Imitation of Christ*, written in the fifteenth century by Thomas à Kempis.

He had no butler, no valet, no racehorse, no yacht, and lived on £2,000 a year for a further ten, rather lonely, years in retirement. He was not interested in personal wealth and always lived very modestly. He once said, "If you have so much money that you can buy anything you want, you find you don't want anything. Nothing gives satisfaction unless you have to struggle for it," adding on another occasion, "Money is only a worry. The best thing you can do is give it away." Maybe at times he did feel a degree of insecurity and the feeling that people only appreciated him for his money, for he once said,

Whatever people may say about me, it is due to my money that every mother in Oxford can have her first baby in hospital.

Sitting in the gardens of Nuffield Place in 1962

The first bicycle he built and bought back for himself years later was one of his most treasured possessions, along with the honorary medal of the Royal College of Surgeons of England.

He is commemorated in the Morris Motors Museum at the Oxford Bus Museum. He has a statue and a building named after him at Guy's Hospital, another building named after him at Coventry University, and a theatre at the University of Southampton. His childhood home in James Street now has a blue plaque. He died in August 1963, aged 85. The baronetcy and two peerages died with him because he was childless. Cremated, Morris' ashes lie in Nuffield churchyard, beside those of his wife. On his death the ownership of his former Oxfordshire home, Nuffield Place, and its contents passed to Nuffield College who opened it to the public on a limited basis. It has now passed to the National Trust and is open to the public on a regular basis.

William Morris (Lord Nuffield) was one of the most remarkable figures of his generation in the UK. His benefactions to Britain and the Commonwealth made him the greatest philanthropist of the twentieth century in Britain who left enduring legacies in medicine, education and welfare.

FURTHER READING

Adeney, Martin. *Nuffield. A Biography* (London: Robert Hale, 1993)

Bardsley, Gillian and Lang, Stephen. *Making Cars at Cowley* (Stroud: Tempus, 2006)

Hunt, Peter. *Lord Nuffield* (London: Shire Publications Ltd, 1993)

Jackson, Robert. *The Nuffield Story* (London: Frederick Muller, 1964)

Minns, F John (ed). *Wealth Well-Given: The Enterprise and Benevolence of Lord Nuffield* (Stroud: Alan Sutton Publishing Ltd, 1994).

Overy, RJ. *William Morris, Viscount Nuffield* (London: Europa Publications Ltd, 1976)

Prioleau, John. *The Adventures of Imshi: A Two-seater in Search of the Sun* (London: Jarrolds, 1922)

APPENDIX
MORRIS CARS (UNTIL HIS DEATH IN 1963)

1913–26 - Morris Oxford bullnose (12 or 14 hp)

1915–31 - Morris Cowley *bullnose and flatnose* (12 or 14 hp)

1923–24 - Morris Oxford Six F series (18 hp)

1926–30 - Morris Oxford flatnose (12 or 14 hp)

1926–29 - Morris Oxford 15.9 and 16/40 (16 hp)

1927–29 - Morris Six (18 hp)

1929–35 - Morris Isis (18 or 25 hp)

1928–32 - Morris Minor (8 hp)

1929–35 - Morris Oxford Six, Sixteen and Twenty (16 or 20 hp)

1931–34 - Morris Cowley (12 or 14 hp)

1931–33 - Morris Major (15 hp then 14 hp)

1932–48 - Morris Ten (10 hp)

1933–35 - Morris Ten Six (12 hp)

1933–35 - Morris Cowley Six (14 hp)

1933–39 - Morris Big Six Twenty-One/Twenty-Five (21 or 25 hp)

1934–39 - Morris Twelve (12 hp)

1935–39 - Morris Fourteen (14 hp)

1935–48 - Morris Eight (8 hp)

1948–52 - Morris Minor MM (8 hp)

1952–56 - Morris Minor

1956–71 - Morris Minor 1000

1948–54 - Morris Oxford MO (14 hp)1948–1953 - Morris Six MS

1954–56 - Morris Oxford series II

1954–59 - Morris Cowley

1955–58 - Morris Isis

1956–59 - Morris Oxford series III

1957–60 - Morris Marshal (BMC Australia)

1958–64 - Morris Major (BMC Australia)

1959–71 - Morris Oxford Farina

1959–69 - Morris Mini Minor

First MG 1925

MGA 1959–62 - 101,000 built 10% coupes 1588cc 98mph price £595

MGB 1965–80 - 500,000 built 24% GT's 1798cc 106 mph price £1217

MGC 1967–69 - 9,000 built 50% GT 2912cc 123 mph price £1383

Other Books by David Cranston available from WORDS BY DESIGN

John Radcliffe and his Legacy to Oxford

David Cranston

978-1-909075-18-4 / 86pp / hb

"Dr Cranston has written a biography, as intriguing as it is scholarly, of one of Oxford's most remarkable benefactors. The incalculable benefits to science, medicine and architecture of Dr Radcliffe's largesse 300 years ago live on to this day and are an eloquent testimony to the vital contribution made by visionary philanthropy to the mission of a university: education, scholarship, research and the public good."

Sir Ivor Crewe, The Master,
University College

I am delighted as a physician to commend a book written by a surgeon about a physician.

Sir Roger Bannister CH

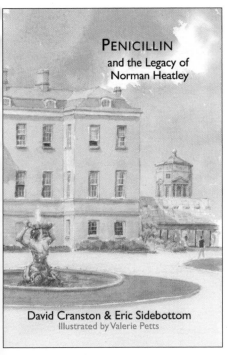

Penicillin and the Legacy of Norman Heatley

David Cranston and Eric Sidebottom

978-1-909075-46-7 / 100pp / hb

"At last, a biography of the crucial member of the Oxford research team that gave the world penicillin."

Professor Max Blythe,
Green Templeton College

"...the most human and humble person you could ever imagine, and his work on the development of penicillin will last for ever."

Paul N. Rimmer, Vicar of Marston, 1959-90

"It is remarkable that while his colleagues were receiving the world's acclaim for the development of penicillin, the crucial contribution of Norman Heatley was largely forgotten. What is equally remarkable is that, in subsequent years, he never expressed even a hint of disappointment or envy at his exclusion."

Sir James Gowans,
Fellow of the Royal Society

WILLIAM OSLER
and his Legacy
to Medicine

David Cranston
Illustrated by Valerie Petts

William Osler and his Legacy to Medicine
David Cranston
978-1-909075-48-1 / 132pp / hb

"William Osler was one of the founding fathers of the Johns Hopkins Hospital. David Cranston's biography will help to keep his name alive, and in these days of increasing technological advance remind all those involved in health care that humanity must remain central, and that, in Osler's own words, 'the patient who has the disease is more important than the disease that has the patient'."

Prof Robert Montgomery, Formerly Director of the Comprehensive Transplant Center, The Johns Hopkins Hospital

John Stott
and The Hookses

David Cranston
with contributions by John Stott,
Chris Wright and Monty Barker